HISTORY UNCUT

THE REAL
King Tut

Virginia Loh-Hagan

45th Parallel Press

Published in the United States of America by Cherry Lake Publishing
Ann Arbor, Michigan
www.cherrylakepublishing.com

Reading Adviser: Marla Conn MS, Ed., Literacy specialist, Read-Ability, Inc.
Book Designer: Felicia Macheske

Photo Credits: © Dundanim/Shutterstock.com, cover, 1; © pgaborphotos/Shutterstock.com, 5, 30; © Jaroslav Moravcik/Shutterstock.com, 7; © Everett Historical/Shutterstock.com, 9; © mountainpix/Shutterstock.com, 11; © Kachaya Thawansak/Shutterstock.com, 12; © Afterfocus Studio/Shutterstock.com, 15; © Waj/Shutterstock.com, 17; © EastVillage Images/Shutterstock.com, 19; © Anton Belo/Shutterstock.com, 20; © Hein Nouwens/Shutterstock.com, 23; © krugloff/Shutterstock.com, 24; © cheapbooks/Shutterstock.com, 27; © Fer Gregory/Shutterstock.com, 29

Graphic Elements Throughout: © iulias/Shutterstock.com; © Thinglass/Shutterstock.com; © kzww/Shutterstock.com; © A_Lesik/Shutterstock.com; © MegaShabanov/Shutterstock.com; © Groundback Atelier/Shutterstock.com; © saki80/Shutterstock.com

45th Parallel Press is an imprint of Cherry Lake Publishing.

Library of Congress Cataloging-in-Publication Data has been filed and is available at catalog.loc.gov

Cherry Lake Publishing would like to acknowledge the work of The Partnership for 21st Century Skills. Please visit www.p21.org for more information.

Printed in the United States of America
Corporate Graphics

Table of Contents

CHAPTER 1

King Tut
The Story You Know

King Tut was a pharaoh. Pharaoh means king. Tut ruled ancient Egypt. Ancient means old. Tut ruled in the 1300s BCE. BCE means "before the Common Era." That means the years before the birth of Jesus.

King Tut ruled during the "New Kingdom." This is a time period in ancient Egyptian history. It was a time of great riches. It was a time of great power. Egypt found gold. It conquered lands. It had a writing system. It traded with other countries. It built large buildings. It built cities.

Tut's tomb was found. He became the most famous pharaoh. But there's more to his story…

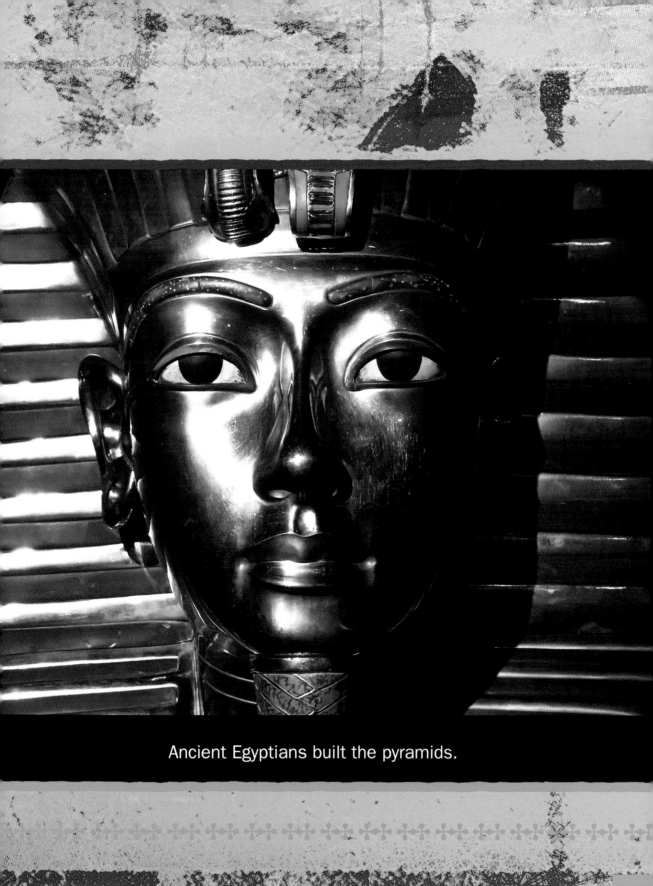

Ancient Egyptians built the pyramids.

CHAPTER 2

Family Man

Ancient Egyptian rulers married family members. They married brothers. They married sisters. They married cousins. They married aunts. They married uncles. This was how ancient Egyptian families stayed in power.

Tut was born a royal prince. His father was Pharaoh Akhenaten. His mother was Akhenaten's sister or cousin. She was one of Akhenaten's many wives. But she was a **minor** wife. She wasn't highly ranked. She's known as "the Younger Lady."

Nefertiti was King Tut's stepmother. She was Pharaoh Akhenaten's top wife. But she didn't have any sons. She only had daughters. So, Tut was the **heir**. Heirs inherit the throne.

Tut came from a family of pharaohs.

SETTING THE WORLD STAGE
1342 BCE – 1320 BCE

▶ In China, the Shang Dynasty ruled at this time. Dynasties are ruling families. The Shang Dynasty laid foundations for Chinese culture. They used the calendar. They started a writing system. They worked with stones and bronze. They lived on farms. They built systems to stop flooding.

▶ Austronesians are people from the Southeast Asia area. They sailed east. They found Fiji around this time. Fiji is a group of islands. They're in the South Pacific.

▶ A citadel is a fortress. Citadel walls were built in Mycenae. Mycenae is in Greece. It was a major city. At this time, 30,000 people lived in the city. There are Greek myths about this city. Perseus was the son of Zeus. Myths say he founded the city. He hired giants called Cyclopes. Cyclopes built the walls. They used giant stones.

"Who you are is limited only by who you think you are."
— Egyptian *Book of the Dead*

Tut married Ankhesenamen. Ankhesenamen was his half-sister. She was the daughter of Nefertiti and Akhenaten. She was older than Tut.

Tut and Ankhesenamen loved each other. They grew up together. They played together. They went to school together. They hunted together. They had 2 daughters. Both their daughters died. Tut's family line ended with him.

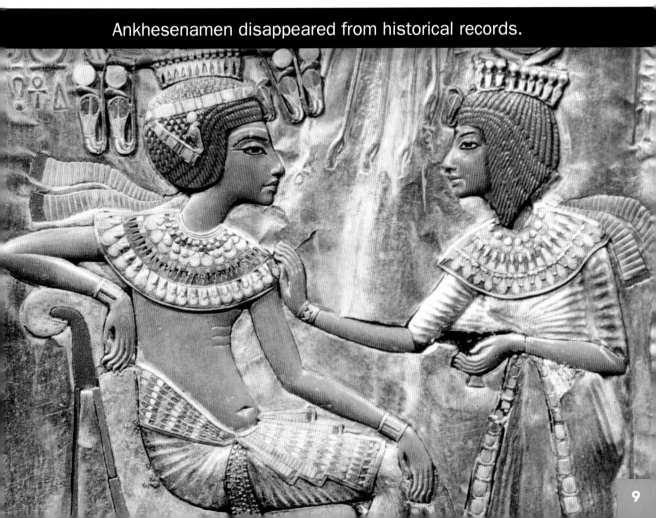

Ankhesenamen disappeared from historical records.

9

CHAPTER 3

Looks Can Be Deceiving

Tut was no Prince Charming. He probably didn't ride horses. He probably didn't fight in battle. He probably looked funny. He had many health problems. This is due to his family **inbreeding**. Inbreeding is when family members have children. Today, doctors tell us inbreeding is bad. Ancient Egyptians didn't know this.

Tut was about 6 feet (183 centimeters) tall. But he wasn't strong. He had a weak body. He was slim. He was frail. He had a bone sickness. His spine wasn't straight. His neck bones joined together. He couldn't move his head.

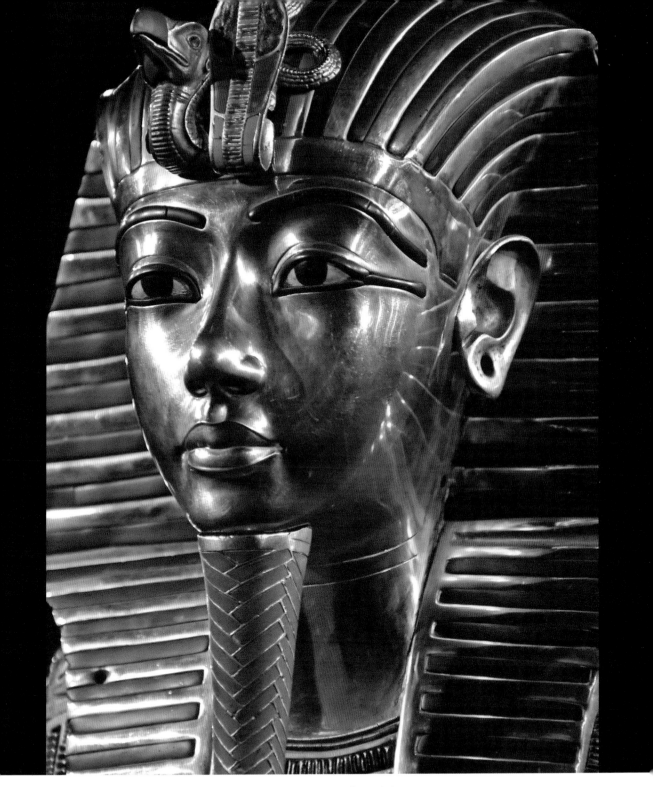

Tut's mask shows a healthy man.

He had a hard time moving. He was born with a **clubfoot**. It's a birth **defect**. Defect is a flaw. One of Tut's feet was smaller than the other. It was rotated. It pointed in. It pointed down. His left foot was rotting. Tut couldn't walk. He had to use canes. He sat for events.

He had large front teeth. He had buckteeth. He had an **overbite**. Overbites are when upper teeth overlap lower teeth. This overbite is a family trait. Many of Tut's family members had overbites.

He also had a **cleft palate**. This is when there's a split in the roof of the mouth. Tut had a hard time eating. He had a hard time talking.

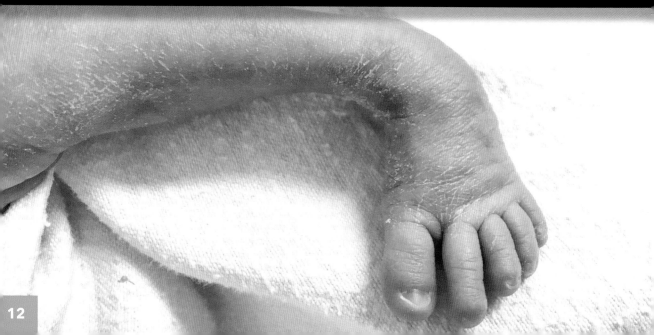
Tut had a clubfoot. There were more than 100 canes in his tomb.

All in the Family

Nefertiti was King Tut's stepmother. She was also his mother-in-law. Nefertiti was Queen of Egypt. She was Pharaoh Akhenaten's wife. She was his chief wife. Her name means "a beautiful woman has come." She had 6 daughters. She's known as the world's first beauty queen. She was beautiful. She had high cheekbones. She's also known as a powerful ruler. She led with her husband. She wore a king's crown. She fought in battle. She supported the worship of 1 god. She supported Aten. Aten was the sun god. Nefertiti ruled during the richest period of ancient Egyptian history. She may have ruled after her husband died. This was before King Tut ruled. But some people deny this. Nefertiti suddenly disappeared from history. No one knows what happened to her. She could've died. Or she could've changed her name. Or she could've run away.

"Details of the room emerged slowly from the mist, strange animals, statues and gold—everywhere the glint of gold." – Howard Carter

CHAPTER 4

The Boy King

Tut's father changed the entire religion of ancient Egypt. Priests were gaining power. They were getting rich. They were equal to pharaohs. Tut's father didn't like this. He stopped it. He changed more than a thousand years of tradition. He forced everyone to worship 1 god. He destroyed old temples. He banned the old gods. He built a new capital city to honor this god.

Tut's father worshipped Aten. Aten was the sun god. He was building a new era. He even named Tut after Aten. Tut was named Tutankhaten. This means "living image of Aten." But many people didn't like the **reforms**. Reforms are changes

14

Tut's father said he spoke for Aten.

THAT
Happened?!?

King Tut had a gold burial mask. It was found in his tomb. It's very valuable. It's more than 3,000 years old. It's now at the Egyptian Museum in Cairo. Cairo is the capital of Egypt. The mask has a beard. The beard is blue and gold. It's braided. Museum workers were fixing the lighting. They accidentally bumped the mask. The mask fell. The beard broke off. Workers tried to fix it. They messed up. They used strong glue. But the glue left a gap. The gap is between the beard and the face. There was glue on the mask. The workers tried to cover up their mistake. They used sharp tools to rub off the glue. They scratched the mask. They damaged it. The workers are in trouble. They're accused of being careless. They're being investigated. Officials say they didn't follow the rules. The museum hired experts to fix the mask.

"When I die, now don't think that I'm a nut. Don't want no fancy funeral. Just one like old King Tut." – Steve Martin

Tut's father died. Then, Tut became pharaoh. He was 9 years old. He ruled for 10 years. Tut rejected what his father did. He worshipped Amun. He let people worship many gods. He changed the capital city back. He restored the old temples. He gave priests some power back.

He changed his name to Tutankhamun. This means "living image of Amun." Amun was the creator god. He ruled the old gods.

Tut had help. People advised him. They helped him rule. They made Egypt a world power. They worked with other kingdoms. They protected their lands. They fought against invaders.

Tut brought harmony back to ancient Egyptians.

CHAPTER 5

Kingly Death

Tut died at a young age. He was still a teenager. No one knows how he died. But scientists studied his remains. They made guesses.

He had a hole in the back of his head. Some think he was murdered. He had an infected broken leg. Some think he got kicked by a horse. Others think he had a **chariot** accident. Chariots are carts. They're pulled by 2 horses. Some think he died of a tooth infection. Some think a hippo killed him.

Scientists found proof of **malaria**. Malaria is a sickness. It's spread by mosquitoes. It could have made Tut weak. It can be deadly.

There are no records of Tut's final days.

Tut was buried in a hurry. His tomb was small. It was too small for a pharaoh. Dark-brown splotches were found on the walls. Tut was buried before the paint dried. This meant his death was not expected.

Tut was turned into a **mummy**. Mummies are wrapped bodies. Ancient Egyptians thought royal bodies should be saved. They saved them for the **afterlife**. Afterlife is what happens after death.

Tut was buried with a golden mask. He was laid in a golden coffin. His tomb had many **chambers**. Chambers are small rooms. They held all types of treasures. This ensured Tut had a safe journey to the afterlife.

Tut was buried in the smallest tomb in the Valley of the Kings.

Bad Blood

King Tut's enemies were the Hittites. The Hittites were from ancient Anatolia. Anatolia is the area now known as Turkey. King Tut had sent his general against the Hittite army. The Hittites were stronger. Egyptian chariots were faster. They only had 2 people. Hittite chariots had 3 people. So, they could shoot more spears. The Hittites and Egyptians were at war from the 15th to 13th centuries BCE. They fought over land. They fought for a long time. They finally made peace. They made the world's first known peace treaty. The Hittites worshipped storm gods. Storm gods were fighters. They supported battles and victories. The Hittites had a strong military. They were good fighters. They used horses. They traveled long distances. They used wheels. They used wagons. They helped develop the Iron Age. They made iron tools. They made iron weapons.

"To be satisfied with a little, is the greatest wisdom. And he that increasth his riches, increasth his care. But a contented mind is a hidden treasure, and trouble findeth it not." – Pharaoh Akhenaten

CHAPTER 6

Opening a Tomb

The front part of Tut's tomb was **looted**. Looted means robbed. This happened soon after Tut was buried. But the inner rooms were sealed. So, the robbers didn't find Tut. Tut's tomb was hidden. Stones covered it. Huts were built over it. It was forgotten. Tut was unknown for more than 3,000 years.

Then, he became world-famous. This happened in 1922. He became the most famous pharaoh of all time.

Howard Carter was a British **archaeologist**. Archaeologists study human history. They do digs. They study **artifacts**. Artifacts are tools and things. They're left behind by people. They're left over time.

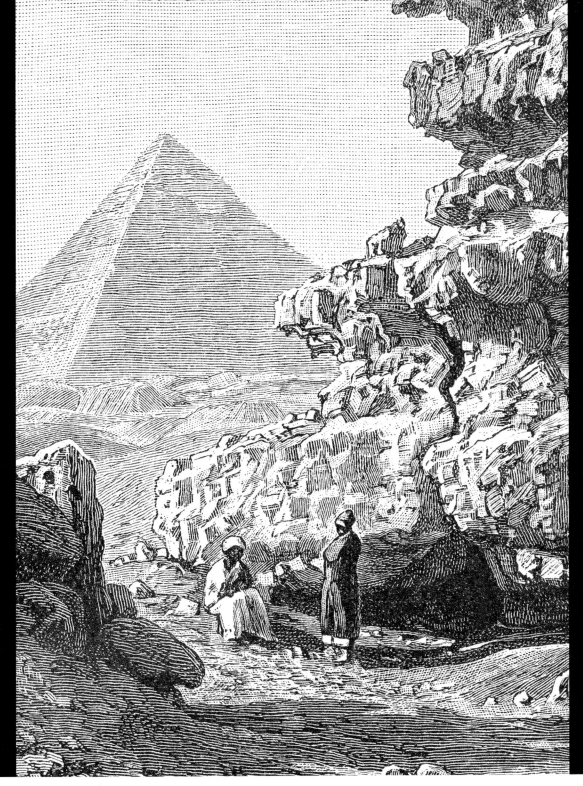

Scientists think Tut's tomb was robbed at least twice in ancient times.

Carter dug and dug. He found Tut's tomb. He found Tut's mummy. He found his treasures. There were about 5,000 artifacts. Carter found Tut's golden mask. He found the golden coffin. He found musical instruments. He found weapons. He found food. He found clothes. He found all kinds of things. It took him 10 years to record everything.

This was an important discovery. Artifacts were sent to museums. People were able to learn about ancient Egypt. They learned about royal life. They learned about the time period.

◀ Carter found a knife made from a meteorite in King Tut's tomb.

CHAPTER 7

King Tut's Curse

A **curse** is a hex. People get mad. They curse others. They wish bad things to happen.

People think King Tut's tomb was cursed. Newspapers spread the idea. They called it the "Curse of the Pharaoh." Carter supported the idea. He wanted to scare people. He wanted to keep people away. He wanted to protect the tomb.

Hieroglyphs are ancient Egyptian writings. There were hieroglyphs on the door of Tut's tomb. People misread the words. They thought the words were a curse. They thought the curse was deadly. Death would come to all those who disturbed Tut.

People were scared of the curse.

Explained by
SCIENCE

Ancient Egyptians embalmed bodies. They mummified the bodies. They saved the bodies. The mummies were homes for spirits. All living things have bacteria. Bacteria are like germs. Embalming doesn't let bacteria get to dead bodies. It doesn't let air in. This stops bodies from rotting away. Ancient Egyptians hired special priests to do this. The priests removed organs. They used a hook to remove the brain. They put the hook up the nose. They pulled out the brain. They left hearts. They put organs in jars. They buried them with the body. They removed water from bodies. They put salt on the bodies. They waited for the bodies to dry out. They washed off the salt. They filled in the body with cloth. They wanted the body to look like the person. They wrapped the bodies. It took 70 days to make a mummy.

"All we have to do is peel the shrines like an onion, and we will be with the king himself." —Howard Carter

Lord Carnarvon paid for the dig. He entered the tomb. He died 4 months after. People thought the curse killed him. But there was a real reason. Doctors said he died of blood poisoning. He got bitten by a mosquito. The bite got infected.

Lord Carnarvon's death inspired the curse story. Several more people who visited the tomb died. This made the curse seem even more real. There were more than 50 people at the tomb. Eight people died. They died within several years of the discovery. Doctors gave a reason for all the deaths.

Tut's death is more famous than his life.

The curse isn't real. But people like believing in it.

Timeline

1342 BCE Tut was born. He had a wet nurse. This is someone who fed him as a baby. Her name was Maia.

1333 Tut became Pharaoh of Egypt. Women rulers were also called pharaohs.

1332 Tut got married.

1331 Tut changed his name. He changed from Tutankhaten to Tutankhamun. He did this to show Amun was more important than Aten.

1330 Tut moved to the old capital of Thebes. This gave back power to Amun's priests.

1325 Tut died.

1324 Tut was buried in a tomb. Priests wrapped his body. They may have hit his head. They were removing his brain.

1922 CE Tut's tomb was discovered by Howard Carter. The tomb was still intact.

Consider This!

Some people think King Tut was just an okay leader. He was more important in death. What do you think? Was King Tut a good leader? Argue your point with reasons and evidence.

Learn more about Howard Carter. Learn more about the discovery of King Tut's tomb. Explain what was found. Explain what we learned about ancient Egypt.

Historians study history. They study primary documents. They study artifacts. They piece together information. Learn more about their job. Talk to a historian. Think about what future historians would say about how we live today.

Learn More

Boyer, Crispin. *Everything Ancient Egypt*. Washington, DC: National Geographic, 2011.

Hyde, Natalie. *King Tut*. New York: Crabtree Publishing Company, 2014.

Levy, Janey. *The Curse of King Tut's Tomb*. New York: Gareth Stevens Publishing, 2015.

Morley, Jacqueline, and David Antram (illust.). *You Wouldn't Want to Be Cursed by King Tut!: A Mysterious Death You'd Rather Avoid*. New York: Franklin Watts, 2011.

Glossary

afterlife (AF-tur-life) the place where people's souls go after dying

ancient (AYN-shuhnt) old

archaeologist (ahr-kee-AH-luh-jist) a scientist who studies human history by doing digs and finding artifacts

artifacts (AHR-tuh-fakts) items that are left behind by people

BCE (BEE SEE EE) "before the Common Era," the time period before Jesus was born

chambers (CHAYM-burz) small rooms

chariot (CHAR-ee-uht) two-wheeled cart pulled by horses

cleft palate (KLEFT PAL-it) a split in the roof of the mouth

clubfoot (KLUHB-fut) a birth defect in which 1 foot is smaller than the other and is rotated inward and downward

curse (KURS) a hex or a promise of evil things to come

defect (dee-FEKT) a mistake

heir (AIR) a person with a legal claim to inheritance

hieroglyphs (hire-uh-GLIF-iks) ancient Egyptian writings

inbreeding (IN-breed-ing) when family members have children

looted (LOOT-id) robbed

malaria (muh-LAIR-ee-uh) a deadly sickness spread by mosquitoes

minor (MYE-nur) lower rank, less than major

mummy (MUHM-ee) a body that is wrapped in order to be preserved over time

overbite (OH-vur-bite) a condition when upper teeth overlap lower teeth

pharaoh (FAIR-oh) an Egyptian king

reforms (rih-FORMZ) changes

Index

About the Author

Dr. Virginia Loh-Hagan is an author, university professor, former classroom teacher, and curriculum designer. She is amazed by the work historians and archaeologists do. She lives in San Diego with her very tall husband and very naughty dogs. To learn more about her, visit www.virginialoh.com.